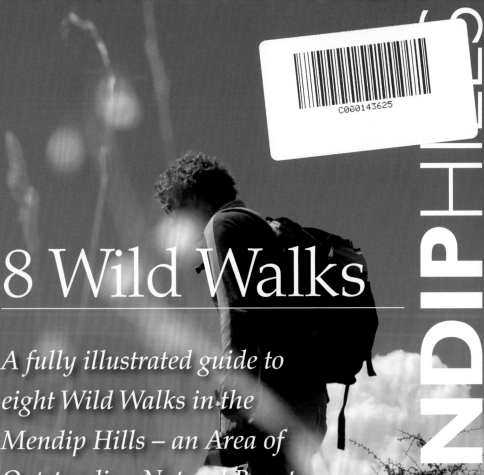

8 Wild Walks

*A fully illustrated guide to
eight Wild Walks in the
Mendip Hills – an Area of
Outstanding Natural Beauty.*

THE MENDIP HILLS

MENDIP HILLS

Area of Outstanding
Natural Beauty

Contents

Contents

Walking the Mendip Hills in safety

All eight Wild Walks in this book are suitable for any reasonably fit person, but the less experienced walker should try the easier routes first. Following the route directions should be straightforward, but you will find that the relevant Ordnance Survey map is a useful addition to the information presented here. Carry a compass as well – just in case you lose your way.

Each walk has been carefully researched to minimise any danger to walkers but it should be stressed that no walk is completey risk-free. Walking in the countryside will always require an element of common sense and judgement to ensure that it is as safe and pleasurable an activity as possible.

Walking is great exercise for people of all ages and the perfect way to keep fit and healthy. For the occasional walker it's not really necessary to spend a fortune on the basic equipment, although a sturdy pair of comfortable boots or shoes and a reliable waterproof jacket is a must. Experienced walkers wear layers of clothing which can be put on or taken off as conditions change. The secret is to maintain a comfortable and even temperature throughout your walk.

Carry a small rucksack with a hat, spare top, gloves and waterproofs, and it's a really good idea to take a drink and some food with you to keep liquid and energy levels up. Walking is exercise, after all, and you'll need to refuel as necessary.

A few words to the wise...

- **Take a few moments to remind yourself of the Countryside Code overleaf.**

- **Our weather is very unreliable and conditions can change quickly. Check the forecast before you set out and ensure that you are equipped with warm and waterproof clothing and appropriate footwear. In the summer months it is advisable to wear a hat and carry sun cream and extra water.**

- **Carry a torch and a fully-charged mobile phone in case of emergencies.**

- **Several of the Wild Walk routes use or cross busy roads. Please be aware that even country lanes and unclassified roads are not traffic-free.**

- **Take particular care on upland areas where the consequences of a slip or fall could be serious.**

The Countryside Code

Be safe – plan ahead and follow any signs

Even when going out locally, it's best to get the latest information about where and when you can go. For example, your rights to go onto some areas of open land may be restricted while work is carried out either for safety reasons or during breeding seasons. Follow advice and local signs and be prepared for the unexpected.

- Refer to up-to-date maps or guidebooks, visit the maps page on the Countryside Access website or contact local information centres.
- Take responsibility for your own safety and for others in your care. Be prepared for changes in weather and other events. Visit the Countryside Directory on the Countryside Access website for links to organisations offering specific advice on equipment and safety, or contact visitor information centres and libraries for a list of outdoor recreation groups.
- Check weather conditions before you leave, and don't be afraid to turn back.
- Part of the appeal of the countryside is that you can get away from it all. You may not see anyone for hours, and there are many places without clear mobile phone signals, so let someone know where you're going and when you expect to return.

Leave gates and property as you find them

Please respect the working life of the countryside, as our actions can affect people's livelihoods, our heritage, and the safety and welfare of animals and ourselves.

- A farmer will normally leave a gate closed to keep livestock in, but may sometimes leave it open so they can reach food and water. Leave gates as you find them or follow instructions on signs. If walking in a group, make sure the last person knows how to leave the gates.
- If you think a sign is illegal or misleading such as a 'Private – No Entry' sign on a public footpath, contact the local authority.
- In fields where crops are growing, follow the paths wherever possible.
- Use gates, stiles or gaps in field boundaries when provided – climbing over walls, hedges and fences can damage them and increase the risk of farm animals escaping.
- Our heritage belongs to all of us – be careful not to disturb ruins and historic sites.
- Leave machinery and livestock alone – don't interfere with animals even if you think they're in distress. Try to alert the farmer instead.

Protect plants and animals and take your litter home

We have a responsibility to protect our countryside now and for future generations, so make sure you don't harm animals, birds, plants or trees.

- Litter and leftover food doesn't just spoil the beauty of the countryside, it can be dangerous to wildlife and farm animals and can spread disease. Please take your litter home with you. Dropping litter and dumping rubbish are criminal offences.
- Discover the beauty of the natural environment and take special care not to damage, destroy or remove features

such as rocks, plants and trees. They provide homes and food for wildlife, and add to everybody's enjoyment of the countryside.

- Wild animals and farm animals can behave unpredictably if you get too close, especially if they're with their young – so give them plenty of space.
- Fires can be as devastating to wildlife and habitats as they are to people and property – so be careful not to drop a match or smouldering cigarette at any time of the year. Sometimes, controlled fires are used to manage vegetation, particularly on heaths and moors between October and early April, so please check that a fire is not supervised before calling 999.

Keep dogs under close control

The countryside is a great place to exercise dogs, but it's every owner's duty to make sure their dog is not a danger or nuisance to farm animals, wildlife or other people.

- By law, you must control your dog so that it does not disturb or scare farm animals or wildlife. On most areas of open country and common land (known as 'access land') you must keep your dog on a short lead between 1 March and 31 July, and all year round near farm animals.
- You do not have to put your dog on a lead on public paths, as long as it is under close control. As a general rule, keep your dog on a lead if you cannot rely on its obedience. By law, farmers are entitled to destroy a dog that injures or worries their animals.
- If a farm animal chases you and your dog, it is safer to let your dog off the lead – don't risk getting hurt by trying to protect it.

- Take particular care that your dog doesn't scare sheep and lambs or wander where it might disturb birds that nest on the ground, or other wildlife – eggs and young will soon die without protection from their parents.
- Everyone knows how unpleasant dog mess is and it can cause infections, so always clean up after your dog and get rid of the mess responsibly. Make sure your dog is wormed regularly to protect it, other animals and people.
- At certain times, dogs may not be allowed on some areas of access land or may need to be kept on a lead. Please follow any signs.

Consider other people

Showing consideration and respect for other people makes the countryside a pleasant environment for everyone – at home, at work and at leisure.

- Busy traffic on small country roads can be unpleasant and dangerous to local people, visitors and wildlife – so please slow down.
- Respect the needs of local people – for example, don't block gateways, driveways or other entry points with your vehicle.
- Keep out of the way when farm animals are being gathered or moved and follow directions from the farmer.
- When riding a bike or driving a vehicle, slow down for horses, walkers and livestock and give them plenty of room. By law, cyclists must give way to walkers and horse-riders on bridleways.
- Support the rural economy – for example, buy from local shops.

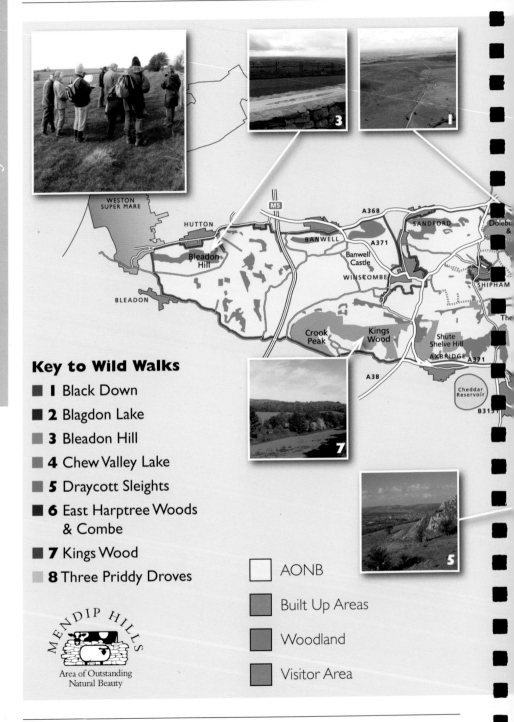

Key to Wild Walks

- **1** Black Down
- **2** Blagdon Lake
- **3** Bleadon Hill
- **4** Chew Valley Lake
- **5** Draycott Sleights
- **6** East Harptree Woods & Combe
- **7** Kings Wood
- **8** Three Priddy Droves

MENDIP HILLS
Area of Outstanding
Natural Beauty

AONB

Built Up Areas

Woodland

Visitor Area

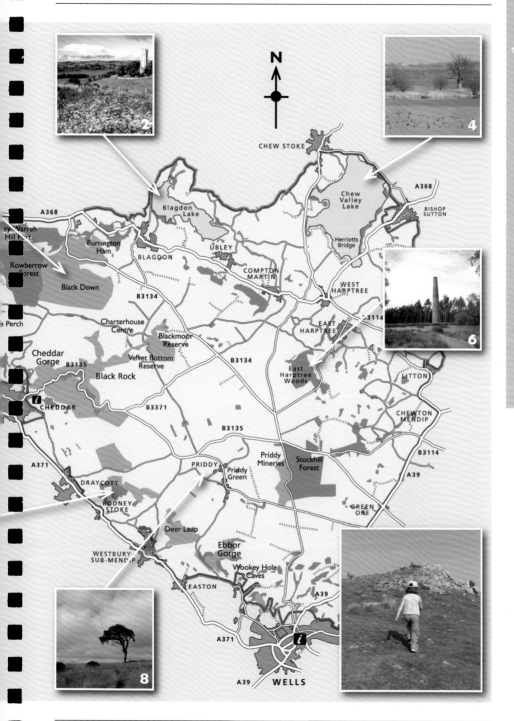

N

CHEW STOKE

Chew Valley Lake

A368

BISHOP SUTTON

Herriotts Bridge

Blagdon Lake

A368

Warren Hill Fort

Burrington Ham

UBLEY

Rowberrow Forest

BLAGDON

COMPTON MARTIN

WEST HARPTREE

Black Down

B3134

EAST HARPTREE

B3114

Perch

Charterhouse Centre

Blackmoor Reserve

B3134

East Harptree Woods

LITTON

Cheddar Gorge

B3135

Velvet Bottom Reserve

Black Rock

CHEWTON MENDIP

i

CHEDDAR

B3371

B3135

Priddy Mineries

Stockhill Forest

B3114

A39

A371

DRAYCOTT

PRIDDY

Priddy Green

GREEN ORE

RODNEY STOKE

Deer Leap

WESTBURY-SUB-MENDIP

Ebbor Gorge

Wookey Hole Caves

A39

EASTON

A371

i

A39

WELLS

BLACK DOWN:
Rescuing an ancient ecology

Heathlands are such important habitats – and so much under threat – that in 1986 all European heathlands were given the protection of the European Union (EU) Habitats Directive.

Heathland is typically a dramatic, open landscape characterised by dwarf shrubs, primarily of the heather family. Black Down, like most heathlands, formed through a combination of factors – soil type, rainfall and human activity.

The combination of the Old Red Sandstone rock which underlies the area and the high rainfall on the Mendips created a waterlogged and acidic soil. The removal of tree cover by our Bronze Age ancestors 2,000 years ago helped to make sure that the soil stayed damp and acid.

Only certain plants can survive in this type of ground. The key species include heather or ling, bell heather, bilberry, purple moor grass and European gorse, along with mosses and lichens.

Heather cutting and grazing have helped to keep the heathland vegetation unchanged for thousands of years, and Black Down is one of the few truly wild landscapes left in the area. Unfortunately, in the last few decades, the abandonment of this traditional management has led to an invasion of scrub and bracken with far less ecological value. Today, the bracken is managed by harvesting with machinery along with grazing by cattle and wild ponies, which is creating more space for the heathers and grasses to flourish again.

Black Down supports a wide variety of birds, mammals, reptiles and invertebrates. One of the key indicators of this is the presence of a healthy population of predatory birds; they are at the top of the food chain, so we know that if they are doing well there must be a strong population of small mammals. In turn, the presence of these mammals tells us that there must be plenty of plant and seed food available.

Mendip Hills AONB Service

Death from fifty feet up

Perhaps our most familiar bird of prey, it is superbly graceful and streamlined. It hovers precisely in the air, then dives from its vantage point in the sky with talons extended, to kill and devour some unsuspecting small mammal.

Not for nothing is the **kestrel** (*Falco tinnunculus*) also known as the windhover. Common and widespread throughout the UK, it is found in a wide variety of habitats including farmland, heathland and urban areas, as well as along motorways and roadsides. The female is slightly larger than the male – both are brown with light undersides but the male has a blue-grey head and tail.

The kestrel's chief prey is small mammals, particularly voles and shrews, but it will also eat insects, worms, other birds – and even bats.

Illustrations: Neil Ross

Heathland plants to look for

Bilberries were picked by our hunter-gatherer ancestors, and are still valued by Scandinavian reindeer herders. In the UK they are often overlooked, but are gathered commercially on a very small scale in some areas, particularly Wales. The fruit is used to make jams and jellies and as an ingredient in summer puddings.

Bilberry or Whortleberry
(*Vaccinium myrtillus*)
Widespread and locally abundant on heaths and moors in the UK. A low shrub

A year in the life of a Kestrel

SPRING
- Kestrels begin to defend their territories and exhibit breeding behaviour – display, courtship and pair formation
- Kestrels do not build their own nests. They use old or disused nests, ledges on cliffs and buildings, or holes in trees and nest boxes
- The weather dictates when the eggs are laid. Normally each pair raises a clutch of 3-6 eggs in late April or early May
- The female lays her eggs at two-day intervals and incubation takes 27-29 days.

SUMMER
- The male provides the female and the chicks with food throughout the nesting period
- Only as the young get bigger will the female start to hunt, close to the nest at first
- The chicks fledge gradually at around four weeks old. They begin to explore the area, gradually ranging further from the nest
- The adult kestrels continue to feed their young for a month after fledging
- The young begin to learn to catch their own food
- Once the young have flown the nest, the adults hunt extensively for themselves.

AUTUMN AND WINTER
- If food is in good supply, the kestrels will stay hunting within their territory.

with hairless twigs 20-50cm high. The leaves are oval and slightly toothed and the small, black fruits appear from July to September.

The many uses of heather

Heather offers much more than a pleasant scent and a lucky charm. In the past it has been used as a roofing material for houses, to make brushes, as a source of fuel, as bedding (for both animals and people), and to make rope and dye. The nectar-rich blossom has also been used to make beer, and the dried flower to make tea.

Ling
(Calluna vulgaris)
Bell heather
(Erica cinerea)

These two common heather species are widespread and abundant on heaths and moors in the UK and give many stretches of upland Britain their characteristic purple shade in late summer. They are both evergreen shrubs 20-100 cm high. The flowers of heather are many and small in opposite rows on spikes, while those of bell heather are larger, bell-shaped and a darker purple. They appear between August and September.

Other things to look out for on Black Down

- Bronze Age burial mounds on Beacon Batch
- Avenues cleared in World War II creating a false airfield designed to confuse enemy aircraft
- Exmoor ponies
- Devon ruby red cattle

Black Down

Distance: 8.5km (5 miles).

Time: About 2-2½ hours.

Starting point: Charterhouse car park, OS Grid Ref ST 502 557.

Terrain: A mixture of uneven bridleways, footpaths and roads, with steep climbs from Charterhouse.

Route 1: From the Charterhouse Centre car park turn right and walk north up the lane and take the second turning left up Rains Batch (1). The lane becomes much steeper here passing a house on the left. From the transmission towers (2), continue west with the towers on your right, and follow track through the gate (3) and up to the trig point on Beacon Batch (4). Continue west on this track until you reach the second intersection (5), then turn sharp left (back on oneself) and head back on the bridleway to the gate you went through earlier (3). Retrace route past the transmission towers (2) into Rains Batch. Take the field entrance just before the house and follow permissive footpath (6) across the fields. Go over the wall stile, through a gate and head south east to the field corner. Go through a gate to the lane opposite the Centre. Follow the lane back to the Charterhouse car park.

Waymarking: Look for the special waymark plaques wherever there are stiles, gates or changes of direction.

O.S. Map: Explorer 141: Cheddar Gorge & Mendip Hills West.

Other Information: Pubs at the bottom of Burrington Combe, at Rickford and in Blagdon. Village post office and stores in Blagdon. Free parking at the village club car park.

Adrian Boots

Adrian Boots

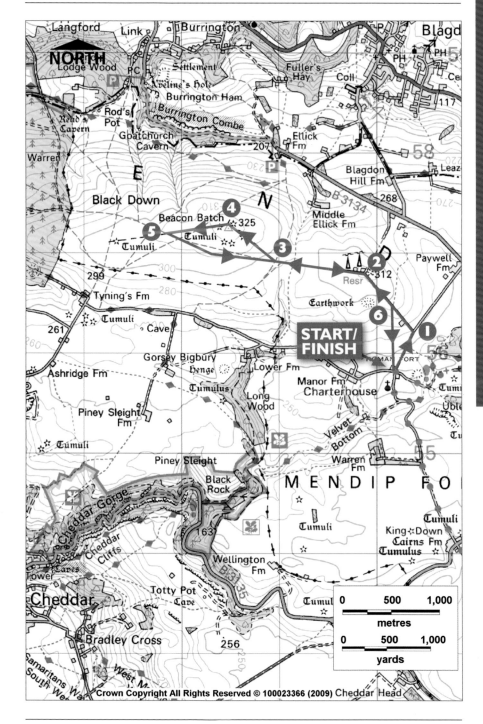

BLAGDON LAKE:
Man-made, adopted by nature

If it weren't for the Victorian dam that runs for a third of a mile along its western end, you could be forgiven for thinking Blagdon was a natural lake. In fact this peaceful 440-acre reservoir has been there so long – the dam was built back in 1891 – that it has long since blended into the landscape of the northern flanks of the Mendips.

Blagdon takes its name from nearby Black Down. The work of building the massive dam took eight years – the larger materials had to be brought in on the Wrington Vale Light Railway Company's branch line. A large Gothic-style building was constructed to house four massive steam-powered beam engines to pump the water. They have now been replaced by electric motors, but two of the original engines were preserved and can still be seen at Blagdon pumping station.

Chris Newton

A rich variety of wildlife soon colonised Blagdon and in more recent times it has been designated a Site of Special Scientific Interest (SSSI). Its meandering 7 miles (11km) of shoreline alternates sheltered bays, reedbeds, carr woodland and grassland. Reed sweet-grass, reed canary-grass and common reed populate the shoreline and there are aquatic plants such as flowering rush and shoreweed.

Species-rich meadows border parts of the north shore and these are home to saw-wort, wild carrot and pepper saxifrage. Many interesting insects, including a wide variety of butterflies and moths, frequent them in summer. The trout which have been stocked by the water company for anglers since the lake was created (predominantly the faster-growing rainbow trout these days) have a rich variety of food to choose from – particularly the larvae of insects such as damselflies, dragonflies, water beetles, midges and sedge flies (caddis flies). There are also sticklebacks, eels, perch and gudgeon.

The lake's rich supply of food ensures a thriving population of waterfowl. They include coot, moorhen, tufted duck, teal, wigeon, mallard, great crested and little grebe, reed bunting, sedge warbler, shoveler, goldeneye, ruddy duck, Bewick's swan, heron and kingfisher.

Devil's darning needles

That's just one of the old country names for dragonflies and damselflies. The two sub-orders are distinguished by the way they hold their wings – those of the dragonflies *(anisoptera)* are held flat like an aeroplane when perching, while the more delicate damselflies *(zygoptera)* bring their wings together.

Several species are common at Blagdon in summer including two of the largest dragonflies, the spectacular southern hawker *(Aeshna cyanea)* and the even larger golden-brown emperor dragonfly *(Anax imperator)*.

The **ruddy darter dragonfly** *(Sympetrum sanguineum)* is locally common in the South of England and widespread at Blagdon (this one was photographed in Rugmoor Bay on the lake's north shore). The mature male has a blood red face and abdomen, with a marked constriction or 'waist' shape to the abdomen. Immature males and mature females have orange-brown abdomens, while both have black legs. They grow up to 35mm in length when mature and fly from mid-June to October.

Paul Glendell/Natural England

Chris Newton

The colourful life story of the ruddy darter

- The juveniles (nymphs) use plant stems to crawl up out of the water in the early morning. The skin then splits to allow the fully-formed adult to emerge
- Mature males occupy perches near breeding sites and defend small territories. They will try another perch if they fail to spot a female

- Females are intercepted as they approach, and the two mate on nearby vegetation
- The female lays her eggs while still in tandem with the male. She dips her abdomen in open water, on vegetation or in mud to deposit the eggs (damselflies may crawl deep into the water to lay their eggs)
- In high summer the eggs hatch within a few days, but if they are laid late in the season they will not hatch until the following spring
- The nymph feeds on the bottom for a year, hiding among the roots of water plants and gradually growing bigger. Small invertebrates and tadpoles are among their food.

Lakeside vegetation to look out for

Common reed *(Phragmites communis)*
This familiar lakeside plant is characteristic of shallow, freshwater margins, wet ground around ponds, marshes, lakes and slow moving rivers. It often forms large beds. When mature, this tall and elegant plant is topped with a large cluster of purple plumes.

The common reed used to be a far more economically important plant than it is now, as this is the plant that is used to make thatch for roofing. It is also home to two bird species which are named after it, the reed warbler and the reed bunting (the latter is common at Blagdon). It is a vital element in the ecology of Blagdon and neighbouring Chew Valley Lake, as it stabilises muddy areas and provides cover for many birds and invertebrates.

Other things to look out for at or near Blagdon Lake

- Blagdon pumping station *(see right)*
- Blagdon Village and Church
- Eldreds orchard

Blagdon Lake

Distance: 4km (2½ miles).

Time: About 1-1½ hours.

Starting point: Free car park next to Blagdon Village Club OS Grid Ref ST 501 591.

Terrain: Some steeper gradients on lanes, otherwise an easy, fairly level route on the footpaths.

Route: From the car park, walk north down through the village (1) – note the lane becomes steeper here. Turn right into Dark Lane (2). At the bottom, turn left (3) along the road towards Blagdon pumping station (4). Follow the road across the dam; at the end on the right there is the entrance to a footpath (5). Take this footpath along the lake shore. At the very northern tip of the lake, look out for a footpath bisecting the path you are on. Take the left path (6) across two fields to Blagdon Lane. Turn left down this lane (7) and return to the dam (8). Retrace the route you have already taken back to the car park.

Waymarking: Look for the special waymark plaques wherever there are stiles, gates or changes of direction.

O.S.Maps: Explorer 141: Cheddar Gorge & Mendip Hills West; Explorer 154: Bristol West & Portishead

Other Information: Pubs in Blagdon: New Inn, Live & Let Live, Seymour Arms and Queen Adelaide. Village post office and stores in Blagdon.

Chris Newton

Richard Law

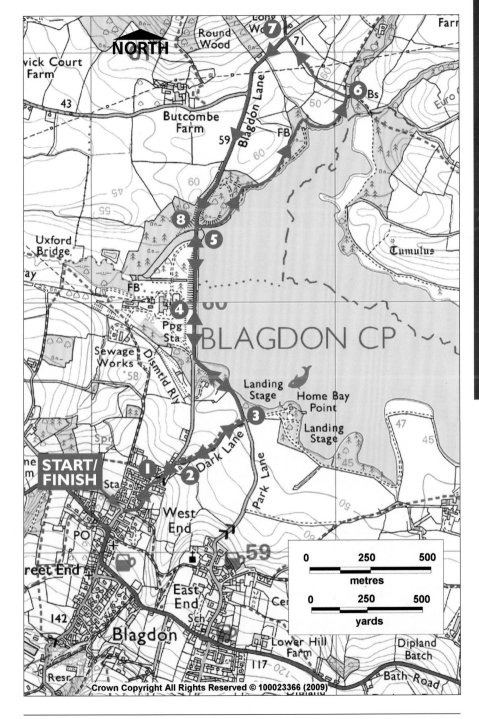

NORTH

Round Wood

Long W 7

71

Farr

ick Court Farm

43

Butcombe Farm

59

Blagdon Lane

60

FB

6 Bs

50

Euro

B

Tumulus

Uxford Bridge

ay

FB

8

5

ne

45

55

60

BLAGDON CP

Ppg Sta

Sewage Works

58

Dismtld Rly

4

Landing Stage

Home Bay Point

Landing Stage

47

45

3

Spr

START/FINISH

Sta

1

2

Dark Lane

Park Lane

45

60

m

West End

71

PO

59

reet End

East End

Sch

Cer

Lower Hill Farm

Dipland Batch

Blagdon

142

Resr

117

120

Bath Road

0	250	500
metres		

0	250	500
yards		

BLEADON HILL:
Where nature has never been threatened by the plough

Limestone grassland is found over thin mineral soils on calcareous rock such as Carboniferous limestone or Dolomitic conglomerate. These unimproved grasslands (meaning that they have never been ploughed, drained or fertilised for agriculture) are characteristic of the southern scarp of the Mendips.

It's the poor quality of these thin soils and their steep, rocky terrain which has saved them for wildlife, because they are not worth cultivating. Instead they have been used for centuries for grazing – traditionally by sheep, though sometimes by cattle – which has helped to keep the turf short.

Bleadon Hill is a mosaic of turf, scrub and woodland characterised by hawthorn, blackthorn and bramble. The grassland is a home to a variety of plants such as sheep's fescue, meadow oat-grass, the rare crested hair-grass, Somerset hair-grass and dwarf sedge, which is nationally scarce. Herbaceous plants such as salad burnet, small scabious and wild thyme, common spotted orchid, pyramidal orchid and bee orchid and the rare spring cinquefoil are also found here.

It is small plants like these which tend to do best here, thanks to the thin soil and the exposed terrain, the tendency for the soil to dry out in summer and the tight grazing by sheep and rabbits.

The grassland is also home to many insects. Butterflies include the small blue, large blue – reintroduced successfully from Sweden a few years ago after becoming extinct in the UK – grizzled skipper, grayling, brown argus and chalkhill blue. Overhead, the majestic buzzard can be seen spiralling on the thermal air currents.

We're lucky to have these grasslands in Somerset as they are nationally rare. That's why Bleadon Hill and neighbouring Shiplate Slait have been designated as Sites of Special Scientific Interest (SSSI), the former for its geology (dry

Mendip Hills AONB Service

valley, calcareous rock and cemented sand and gravel formations) and the latter for its important variety of wildlife, including rare grasses and herbs.

The flying chequerboard

The wings of the **grizzled skipper** (*Pyrgus malvae*) have a distinctive brown and white chequerboard pattern which makes this lively little butterfly easy to distinguish from other species – except perhaps the chequered skipper, which is no longer found in England. In common with others of its family, the grizzled skipper takes off at great speed and flies in a rapid zigzag, which makes its flight hard to follow. Only when it puts on the brakes and basks on a leaf, a flower or an exposed rock with its wings open can it be observed and clearly identified.

Chris Newton

The grizzled skipper is found on chalk downland sites and sunny woodland rides, as well as unimproved limestone grassland. Like many butterflies it is far less common than it used to be, having declined almost everywhere in the UK during the second half of the 20th century. Its foodplants include cinquefoil, wild and barren strawberry, dog rose, tormentil, salad burnet and bramble blossom, while the adult favours nectar from a variety of flowers including bird's foot trefoil and bugle.

These butterflies occur in small colonies of less than 100 adults. This is a warmth-loving butterfly, and both males

A year in the life of a grizzled skipper

- The female lays her eggs singly, usually in May or June, on the underside of a leaf of the foodplant
- On hatching the caterpillar eats through the egg, then moves to the upper side of the leaf, where it spins a web of silk to protect it while it feeds
- The larva feeds mainly in the early morning and evening. When the leaf is finished it moves to a new one, creating a new web. As it gets bigger it builds a larger shelter by spinning leaves together
- The larva spends a great deal of time resting between feeds, and moults four times as it grows
- The larval stage lasts approximately two months. When fully grown at a length of about 16mm, the caterpillar constructs a loose cocoon at the base of the food plant. It pupates within the cocoon, where it will stay for the next nine months
- The following spring the butterfly emerges from the pupa, pumps fluid into the veins of its wings until they are fully functional, and climbs on to the vegetation to take flight.

and females bask in the sun for long periods, typically on exposed rock and leaves of plants. Males are territorial and will chase any species of butterfly from its territory. Female grizzled skippers entering its territory are courted and if the female is receptive, mating occurs.

The butterfly may appear any time from April to June or even July, and very occasionally there is a second brood in August. The example above was photographed in the Blackmoor nature reserve at Charterhouse on Mendip.

Grassland flowers with a history

Creeping cinquefoil (*Potentilla reptans*) is a creeping perennial, widespread and common in grassland, with 5-7 lobed leaves on long stalks. The five-petalled, yellow flowers are 17-25mm across and appear between June and August. Like many wild flowers which were once considered useful for medicinal purposes it is known by a variety of country names, including 'creeping jenny' and 'five fingers'.

Tormentil (*Pontilla eracta*) is a close relative of the cinquefoil and looks rather similar, but has four petals in its 7-11mm flowerhead rather than five. The unstalked leaves are trifoliate and the flowers appear May to September. The name actually means 'torture', reflecting the use of tormentil to ease colic – the roots would be boiled in milk to make a medicine.

What to see near Bleadon Hill & Shiplate Slait

- Superb views of the Somerset Levels, Moors and coast
- Brent Knoll
- Saxon manorial boundary

Bleadon Hill & Shiplate Slait

Distance: 12km (7½ miles).

Time: About 2½-3½ hours.

Starting point: Bleadon Hill, OS Grid Ref ST 358 578.

Terrain: Mostly uneven bridleways and footpaths with some long steep slopes. Some walking along level lanes.

Route: From the car park on Bleadon Hill, follow lane eastward and take bridleway (**1**) towards Christon Plantation. (**2**) Turn right, then right again and follow the bridleway down Shiplate Slait (**3**). Do not bear left down the West Mendip Way bridleway. Turn right on to track (**4**) and bear left towards the road near Shiplate Manor Farm (**5**). Cross the main road onto the footpath and bear right, westward (**6**), towards Southhill Farm and Bleadon. Enter the farmyard, turning right before footpath sign on wall and pick up the path on South Hill (**7**). Cross the main road towards Wonderstone (**8**) and head up Hellenge Hill (**9**) until you meet the lane at the top of Bleadon Hill (**10**). Go left along the lane, then right through the houses, and bear right along the eastward footpath through the fields along Hutton Hill (**11**). Walk through the woods at the end until you join the lane at Upper Canada (**12**). Turn sharp right (south-west), and walk back up the lane towards the car park.

Waymarking: Look for the special plaques wherever there are stiles, gates or changes of direction.

O.S.Map: Explorer 153: Weston-super-Mare & Bleadon Hill.

Other Information: Pub in Bleadon: Queens Arms.

Peter Roworth/Natural England

Illustration: Neil Ross

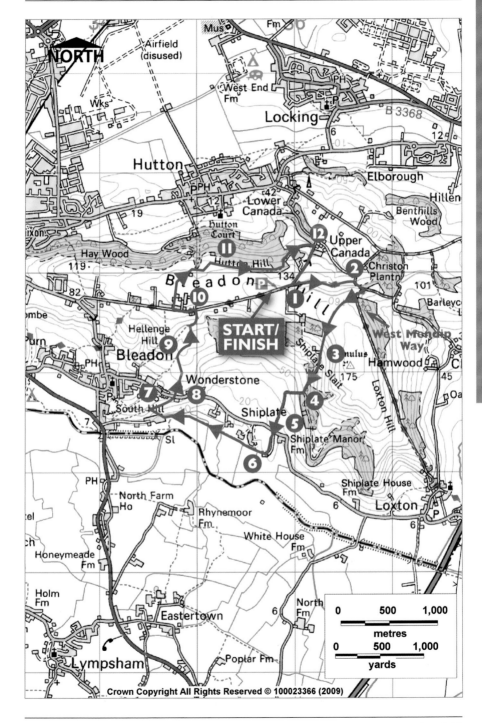

CHEW VALLEY LAKE:
A birdwatcher's paradise

Peter Roworth/Natural England

The largest lake in south-west England, Chew Valley Lake was created in the 1950s as a water supply reservoir for Bristol. In the half century since this 1200-acre lake was created, it has acquired such importance for its natural history that it has been classified as a Site of Special Scientific Interest (SSSI) and a Special Protection Area (SPA).

The lake's 10 miles of shallow and reedy shoreline supports a huge population of waterfowl and other birds – more than 260 species (one of the longest lists of birds recorded at any inland site in the UK) have been recorded here.

The southern end around Herriotts Bridge is a nature reserve where islands, lagoons, bays and channels have been created to provide safe areas for birds to roost, nest, feed and shelter.

The rich waters of the lake teem with aquatic insects and water plants, which provide both protection and food. More than 30 species of mammals live around its shores, including numerous species of bat as well as the occasional otter.

The level of the lake falls by several feet during most summers, to be replenished by winter rainfall. In spring, Chew becomes home to birds returning from hotter climates and those looking for somewhere to mate, nest and breed. The greatest variety of birdlife is recorded in the autumn, when many species stop over on their journey south.

The stately mute swan

The **mute swan** (*Cygnus olor*) breeds in lakes and slow-flowing rivers across the UK. Its long neck helps it to reach aquatic vegetation from the bed of the lake. It also eats grass, worms, small fish and even frogs.

The mute swan has long enjoyed a special status as a royal bird. Every year, an official swan keeper appointed by the Queen carries out a symbolic ceremony on the Thames, which also has a practical use in monitoring the swan's health and numbers.

A pair of swans will mate for life, although (contrary to popular opinion) if one of the birds dies the remaining swan will often find another mate.

A year in the life of a mute swan

SUMMER
- The female (the pen) builds the nest in a suitable waterside location while the male (the cob) hunts for sticks, rushes and dried grasses as nesting material
- Between late April and early May, the female lays up to seven eggs. The parents take it in turns to incubate them and they hatch after 35-41 days
- The fluffy chocolate-brown cygnets stay with their parents for 4-5 months, often riding on their parents' backs.

AUTUMN AND WINTER
- During late autumn or winter the cygnets' plumage becomes predominantly white, at which point the adults begin to drive them away. Some young birds will travel with their parents to join the flocks in an overwintering area.

SPRING
- When the adults return to the breeding area the following spring, the young birds will stay with the flock. They begin to breed at two years old.

Chris Newton

Adrian Boots

Other wildfowl to look out for

Chew Valley Lake's plethora of waterfowl species includes snipe (common and jack snipe), lapwing, teal, wigeon, pochard, mallard, tufted duck, shelduck, goldeneye, coot, moorhen, ruddy duck and shoveler. The secretive water rail is found here, while in winter you might be lucky enough to see – or hear – the rare bittern in the reed beds. Raptors seen regularly include the hobby and the peregrine falcon, and in spring and summer there are countless songbirds.

Wild flowers of Chew Valley

Devil's bit scabious (*Succisa pratensis*) grows in damp meadows and marshes. Its rounded blue-purple flowerheads provide a rich source of nectar for insects from August through to October. It is important as the food plant of the marsh fritillary, one of our most rapidly-declining butterflies, which is still locally common in the Mendips.

The plant got its name from the legend that the devil bit off its root. Devil's bit scabious has the reputation for being able to cure any illness. Tea made from the plant is said to help in the treatment of coughs, fevers and internal inflammations, and it is also reputed to ease skin conditions such as scabies – hence the name.

Cowslip (*Primula veris*) is a close relative of the primrose. It is one of our most familiar country plants and goes by many other local names, including bunch of keys, fairy bells, tisty-tosty, mayflower and palsywort. Less poetically, the standard name is derived from 'cowslop', an old form of 'cowpat'.

The familiar bright yellow, scented

Adrian Boots

flowers – which can be seen in enormous numbers on some roadside embankments – make a delicate country wine, and the plant was used traditionally to treat rheumatism, paralysis and cramps.

Other attractive waterside flowers to watch out for

- Orchids (common spotted, marsh and heath spotted)
- Purple loosestrife
- Yellow flag
- Marsh marigold

Other things to look out for at or near Chew Valley Lake

- Drowned Roman villa and road – when the level is low in the late summer you may be able to see the roadway and humpback bridge from Heron's Green on the west shore.
- The lake is an internationally important trout fishing venue and has a fleet of motor boats for anglers, who may be seen most days from March to October casting their flies for the rainbow and brown trout, of which around 40,000 are caught each season.

Other information

- Woodford Lodge on the north-western shore has a restaurant, bar, toilets and tackle shop.
- There is a tea shop and a picnic area on the north side of the lake.

Chew Valley Lake

Distance: 8km (5 miles).

Time: About 2-2½ hours.

Starting point: Herriotts Bridge, OS Grid Ref ST 571 581.

Terrain: Uneven footpaths, mostly level with little in the way of slopes. Footpath can be very boggy in places. Mostly level, easy going lanes. Take care when crossing A368.

Route: Starting from Herriotts Bridge car park, follow the footpath north-east alongside the A368 and turn right down the lane (1) towards North Widcombe. Opposite the cottages, turn right (2) and follow the marked footpath along the back of Herriotts Mill Pool (3). This section of the footpath can get very boggy so be prepared to walk around any problem areas. Continue along waymarked footpath (4) until you reach West Harptree. Turn right into Whistley Lane (5). Walk past the village shop, cross the A368 and bear right on to the B3114 (6). After 200m look for the public footpath sign (7) and turn right following waymarked path (8) to Stratford Lane. Bear right and walk to the end of Stratford Lane (9), turn right and follow marked footpath to Lower Gurney Farm (10). Cross A368, take footpath opposite and rejoin path behind Herriot's Pool (11), turning left to return to car park.

Waymarking: Look for the special waymark plaques wherever there are stiles, gates or changes of direction.

O.S.Map: Explorer 141: Cheddar Gorge & Mendip Hills West.

Other Information: Ice Cream van at Herriotts Bridge car park. Pub and village shop at West Harptree.

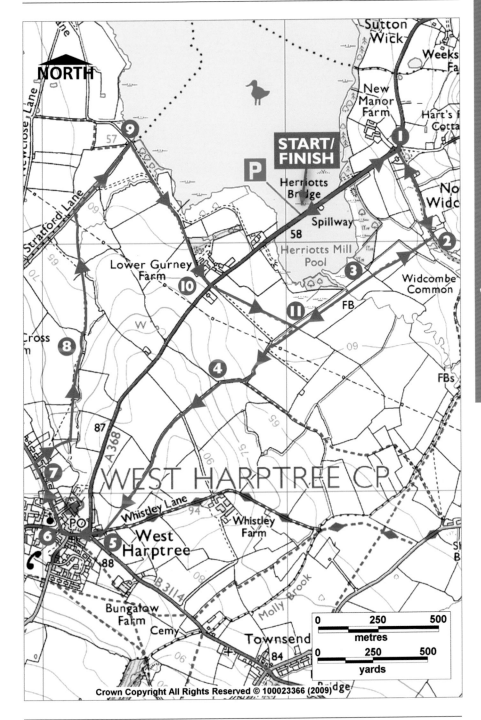

NORTH

Sutton Wick

Weeks Fa

New Manor Farm

Hart's Cotta

1

START/ FINISH

P

Herriotts Bridge

No
Widc

Spillway

58

2

Herriotts Mill Pool

3

Widcombe Common

9

57

Stratford Lane

Lower Gurney Farm

10

11

FB

09

Cross

8

4

FBs

87

A 368

WEST HARPTREE CP

75

90

7

Whistley Lane

94

Whistley Farm

S
B

POS

6

5

West Harptree

88

B 3114

08

Molly Brook

Bungalow Farm

Cemy

Townsend

84

0	250	500
metres		

0	250	500
yards		

dge

DRAYCOTT SLEIGHTS:
A naturalist's paradise

Calcareous (chalky) soils over limestone give rise to a characteristic grassland rich in flowers, sedges and grasses, along with many insects and birds which are rarely found elsewhere. In the right climate the result can be a naturalist's paradise.

Draycott Sleights, south east of Cheddar, is a prime example. The sunny south-facing scarp, with its steeply-sloping

grassland, rocky outcrops and limestone cliffs, provides the perfect habitat for many fascinating plants and invertebrates – all against the backdrop of one of the finest panoramas in Somerset.

The grassland is rich in herbs such as kidney vetch and yellow rattle in the spring, followed in summer by pyramidal and greater butterfly orchids. Search among the limestone cliffs and outcrops and you'll find delicate ferns and the contrasting yellow, white and grey patches of lichens. You might even spot the rare and delicate Cheddar pink.

Wood sage, wall lettuce, dog's mercury and herb robert are present in the loose rocks of the scree slopes. The many grasses and sedges include quaking grass, upright brome, crested hair-grass and sedge, while more open parts of the site are dominated by sheep's fescue and meadow oat-grass. Among them you may find rarer treasures, such as the green-winged orchid (see page 25).

This wealth of flowers, particularly knapweed, scabious and wild marjoram, attract butterflies such as the marbled white, the brown argus, the common blue and the chalkhill blue, whose bright silvery-blue form can be numerous here in late July and August.

The many grasshoppers and crickets include the mottled grasshopper, oak bush-cricket, dark bush-cricket and great green bush-cricket – one of our largest insects. You may be lucky enough to spot the nationally scarce rufous grasshopper.

Dragonflies such as the southern hawker are also present, as are many species of snail. The natural caves and fissures in the limestone are home to the nationally rare greater and lesser horseshoe bats. Other mammals include badgers, brown hares, roe deer and the diminutive muntjac, an introduced species.

Look for patches of sheltered sunny turf close to thick cover and you may spot the black zigzag of a basking adder.

Jim Hallett/Countryside Agency

Mendip Hills AONB Service

Adders are wary creatures which try to bite only if cornered or trodden on – fortunately they can detect the average walker's boots from many yards away, and all you'll notice is the rustle in the grass as they make themselves scarce. Creep along quietly on a sunny spring morning, however, and you may have a chance to observe one properly before it realises you are there. You may also spot the secretive slow-worm.

The many birds to be seen on the Sleights include a wide range of raptors, including buzzards, tawny and little owl, kestrels and peregrine falcons.

This site has been managed for hundreds of years by sheep-grazing ('sleight' means sheep pasture). Limestone grassland that hasn't been 'improved' by modern agriculture is increasingly difficult to find, which is why Draycott Sleights is designated a Site of Special Scientific Interest (SSSI).

Grasshoppers – the Olympic athletes of the insect world

Grasshoppers feed on grasses, leaves and cereal crops. The adults have two pairs of wings and their long hind legs are adapted for jumping – something they are spectacularly good at. The average grasshopper can jump 20 times its own length and reach a speed of 12 feet per second, the equivalent of a human taking off at 600 miles per hour.

Female grasshoppers are larger than the males, reaching around 3cm in length in the bigger species, and have sharp points to their abdomens (ovipositors) for egg laying. It's the males which rub their wings on their hind legs to make the classic sound of summer grassland (crickets do it by rubbing one wing against the other).

Grasshoppers are active both by day and night, but are solitary and only come together to mate. Their many enemies

Grasshopper facts

- There are some 18,000 species of grasshoppers and crickets in the world, most native to hot countries – only about 30 are found in Britain
- You can tell a grasshopper from a cricket by the antennae – those of the grasshopper are short and bristle-like, while crickets have long flexible ones which are often much longer than their bodies
- A grasshopper has five eyes
- A grasshopper can get through 16 times its own body weight in a day
- When the female lays her eggs, she covers them with a paste-like liquid to keep them safe during the winter
- Grasshopper young (nymphs) take 40-60 days to become adults
- The crop-devouring locust is a member of the grasshopper family.

include beetles, birds, mice, snakes and spiders.

Limestone Grassland plants to look out for

An orchid you can smell...

Green-winged Orchid (*Orchis morio*) Most limestone grassland plants are virtually scentless, but the green-winged orchid is distinguished not only by its beautiful blooms, the sepals delicately tinged with green, but its unusual vanilla scent.

This orchid, found from April to June, has 7-8 blue-green, unmarked glossy leaves and one or two pointed leaves that sheathe the flowering stem. The flowers vary in colour from lilac to pinkish-purple, borne on small spikes. The upper petals have dark veins running through them while the lower 'lip' has a red dotted pale patch in the centre. Green winged orchids are pollinated by the red-tailed bumblebee and the bumblebee.

Peter Wakely/Natural England

...and a flower you can hear

Yellow rattle
(Rhinathus minor)
The yellow rattle was once called 'baby's rattle' because of the noise made by the fruits inside the calyx if you shake the plant when it's fully ripe.

A plant of undisturbed, unimproved grassland, the yellow rattle is semi-parasitic. The flower has a black spotted stem that carries opposing pairs of narrow, light green, spear-shaped and toothed leaves. The bright yellow flowers (May-September) are 10-20cm long with hooked upper lips.

Other things to look out for at or near Draycott Sleights

- Amazing views of the Somerset Levels & Moors
- Glastonbury Tor
- Gliders
- Dry stone walls
- Draycott Sleights Nature Reserve

Draycott Sleights

Distance: 4.8km (3 miles).

Time: About 1½-2 hours.

Starting point: Draycott, OS Grid Ref ST 477 510.

Terrain: Mostly uneven bridleways and footpaths with some long steep slopes. Some walking along level lanes.

Route: From Draycott village centre, follow footpath alongside the road towards Cheddar. Bear right **(1)** and after 200m take the bridleway right **(2)**, past Batcombe Farm **(3)**. Follow the bridleway up past Batcombe Hollow **(4)**. Look out for the bridleway junction, take the right hand route **(5)** and follow this into the reserve **(6)**. Follow the bridleway, crossing New Road **(7)**, until you meet the West Mendip Way **(8)**. Follow the West Mendip Way downhill to Sun Batch **(9)** and pick up the lane back into the village.

Waymarking: Look for the special waymark plaques wherever there are stiles, gates or changes of direction.

O.S. Map: Explorer 141: Cheddar Gorge & Mendip Hills West.

Other Information: Pubs in Draycott: Strawberry Special & The Red Lion

Peter Wakely/Natural England

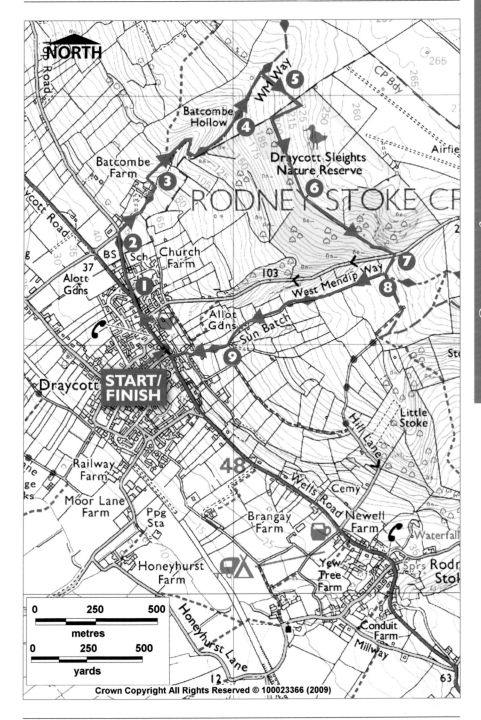

NORTH

Batcombe
Hollow

WM Way

5

4

Batcombe
Farm

3

RODNEY STOKE C

Draycott Sleights
Nature Reserve

2

BS

Sch

Church
Farm

6

37

Alott
Gdns

1

103

7

West Mendip Way

8

Allot
Gdns

Sun Batch

9

**START/
FINISH**

Draycott

Little
Stoke

Hill Lane

Railway
Farm

48

Wells Road

Cemy

Moor Lane
Farm

Ppg
Sta

Brangay
Farm

Newell
Farm

Waterfall

Yew
Tree
Farm

Rodr
Stol

Honeyhurst
Farm

Sprs

Conduit
Farm

Millway

63

| 0 | 250 | 500 |
metres

| 0 | 250 | 500 |
yards

Honeyhurst Lane

12

Crown Copyright All Rights Reserved © 100023366 (2009)

EAST HARPTREE WOODS & COMBE:
Where ancient forest meets young woodland

Most coniferous woodlands in Britain have been planted for forestry purposes – as a crop which will one day be harvested as timber. Because conifers can grow up to six times faster than broadleaved trees, conifer plantations produce much higher yields of timber than slower-growing broadleaf woodlands. Conifer timber is known as softwood and is used for a huge range of products, from paper to furniture. Characteristically, conifer plantations tend to be planted at high density, which reduces the amount of light reaching the woodland floor. Broadleaf woods usually allow far more light through, which leads to a greater diversity of ground flora.

Among conifers only the Scots pine, yew and juniper are considered native to Britain, and most of our conifer plantations are made up of commercially-useful introduced species such as the Douglas fir and the sitka spruce. Like most conifers these species are evergreen, so they do not shed their needles in winter.

East Harptree Woods is a relatively new conifer plantation which has been designed and managed with wildlife in mind. It has a wide ride (open, tree-free space) to link areas of natural vegetation, such as heath and grassland. Once the area was important for lead and zinc mining, and the undulating terrain, known as 'gruffy ground', indicates old pits and spoil heaps. Much of the ore was processed and smelted at this site and you can see the restored Smitham Chimney today.

In front of the chimney there is grassland, heath and a pond where dragonflies flit in the summer months.

Connected to the north-eastern end of the woods is a narrow gorge with a small stream running down. This is Harptree Combe, a Site of Special Scientific Interest (SSSI) for its rich flora and fauna. In contrast to the conifers, this area contains deciduous oak and ash woodland, with old hazel coppice and rough, marshy grassland. The ash and hazel woodland here is rich in interesting ground flora with plants such as bluebell, dog's-mercury, herb paris, autumn crocus

Mendip Hills AONB Service

and yellow archangel, and ferns such as scaly male fern, hart's tongue (see overleaf) and broad buckler fern as well as many moss and fungus species.

A wild walk in this area is an opportunity to enjoy the meeting of two contrasting but equally interesting wildlife habitats and to appreciate the contrast between young coniferous plantation and old ash, oak and hazel woodlands.

Tracking the secretive badger

Chris Newton

Badger *(Meles meles)*
The badger's short but powerful limbs and strong claws, small head and eyes, short thick neck and wedge-shaped body make it perfectly adapted to underground living. The word 'badger' is believed to come from the French word 'bêcheur', meaning digger.

Badgers live in social groups called clans, each roaming over a home range which is large and varied enough to provide a reliable food supply. They are omnivores, eating both animal and plant items. Their staple food is earthworms, which they consume in enormous quantities. They particularly relish the young of mammals such as rats, squirrels and rabbits, and often dig the latter out of their underground stops, working by their exceptionally keen sense of smell. Frogs,

The lifecycle of the badger

- Badgers use a phenomenon known as delayed implantation to ensure that whatever time of year the female is fertilised, birth is delayed until the following February (or thereabouts) so that the cubs have the best chance of survival. Actual development in the womb is only 7 weeks
- Commonly, there are 2 to 4 cubs in each litter
- The cubs do not open their eyes or gain their milk teeth until they are six weeks old
- Fewer than half the cubs born will survive to adulthood
- Cubs do not leave the sett until they are about 8 weeks old
- Once they leave the sett they can hunt for food and no longer rely on the sow's milk for nourishment
- Though mortality in the first two years is very high, those that do survive may live to be as old as 10 years or more.

reptiles and birds are welcome additions to the diet when available, as are bee and wasp larvae, beetles, berries, cereals, nuts, seeds and fungi.

Secretive and nocturnal as badgers are (particularly where disturbed by man), the signs of their presence are easy enough to spot if you know what to look for. They are creatures of habit, relying on scent for navigation, and will repeatedly use the same meandering routes across fields and woods, wearing narrow pathways like miniature sheep tracks. In addition to the very obvious spoil heaps beside their setts, look for their distinctive, broad five-toed footprints (dogs and foxes have only four), their claw marks on trees and their latrine pits.

By any other name...

Bee Nettle, Dumb Nettle and Yellow Dead Nettle are all Somerset names for the distinctive **yellow archangel** *(Lamiastrum galeobdolon)*, a hairy

perennial of woodland and hedgerows. This attractive plant grows up to 45cm in height, with nettle-like leaves that are toothed and oval. The bright yellow flowers are arranged in whorls around the stem above pairs of leaves and can be seen from May to June.

Hart's tongue fern

It's not hard to see how the **hart's tongue fern** *(Phyllitis scolopendrium)* got its name – the leaf is exactly the shape of a deer's tongue. This evergreen plant of damp, shady woods and banks

grows in clumps. The fronds are bright green, undivided, and taper to a point with a heart-shaped base. Underneath the fronds, dark brown spore cases are found in rows. The spores ripen from July to August.

Other points of interest around East Harptree Woods & Harptree Combe

• Prehistoric ochre mine
• Smitham lead mine chimney
• Views of the Chew Valley
• Richmont Castle

East Harptree Woods & Combe

Distance: 6km (3¾ miles).

Time: About 1½-2 hours.

Starting point: East Harptree Woods car park, OS Grid Ref ST 557 541.

Terrain: Uneven tracks, footpaths and lanes, with some steeper slopes.

Route: From car park **(1)**, follow the forestry track north-westerly though woods. Bear left **(2)**, then right **(3)**, then join a path **(4)** from the left. Continue to the open area near the chimney and pond **(5)**. Walk out of the woods, cross the field and turn left before the lane onto the Monarch's Way footpath **(6)**. Continue northwards to the lane, and walk left for a few metres. Take the path on the right **(7)** to Harptree Combe **(8)**. Cross the first path that bisects it and take the second path that joins from the right **(9)**. Follow this uphill towards East Harptree. Where a footpath crosses near the houses **(10)**, carry straight on through the fields (beware of grazing animals) until you rejoin the lane **(11)**. Turn right and left back on to the Monarch's Way footpath until point **(6)** is reached. Turn left and right on to the lane **(12)** and return to the car park.

Waymarking: Look for the special waymark plaques wherever there are stiles, gates or changes of direction. This route follows part of the Monarch's Way footpath.

O.S.Map: Explorer 141: Cheddar Gorge & Mendip Hills West.

Other Information: Parking and picnic area in East Harptree Woods. Pub and village shop in East Harptree.

Adrian Boots

Mendip Hills AONB Service

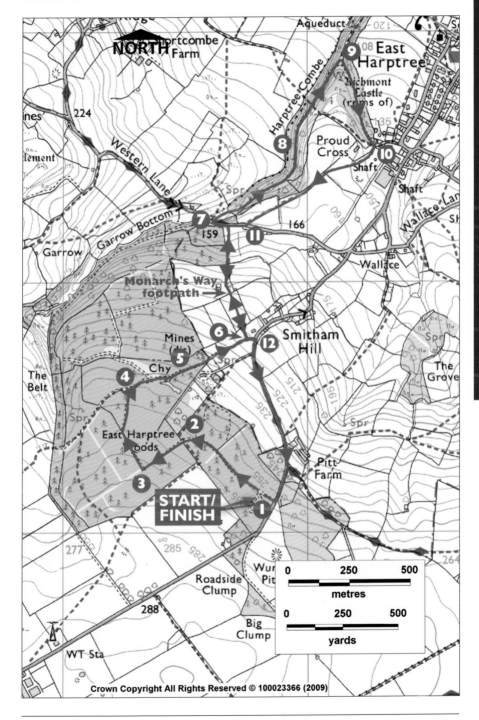

NORTH

Aqueduct

East Harptree

Richmont Castle (rems of)

Harptree Combe

9

Proud Cross

8

10

Shaft

Shaft

224

Western Lane

ines

lement

Spr

166

Wallace Lane

Sh

Garrow Bottom

7

159

11

Wallace

Garrow

Monarch's Way footpath →

Smitham Hill

The Grove

Mines (dis)

6

5

12

Spr

Chy

4

The Belt

Spr

East Harptree Woods

2

3

START/ FINISH

1

Pitt Farm

277

285

Roadside Clump

Wur Pit

Big Clump

288

WT Sta

0	250	500

metres

0	250	500

yards

Crown Copyright All Rights Reserved © 100023366 (2009)

KING'S WOOD:
Ancient woodland with a royal history

The term 'ancient woodland' is generally applied to woods which are believed to have been around since at least AD1600, meaning that there has been continuous woodland cover for over 400 years. Ancient woodland is identified by the UK Biodiversity Action Plan as broadleaved woodland which typically supports almost twice as many wildlife species as any other habitat.

Today, through forest clearance, the rise of agriculture and the march of industry, most of our truly ancient woods have long gone. Fortunately some pockets remain – and King's Wood is among them.

This is one of many woods which formed part of medieval royal hunting forests ('forest' does not strictly mean an area covered in trees – it refers to the use of the land for hunting). King's Wood has a medieval ditch and bank to protect it and is bordered by part of an even older Saxon manorial boundary.

The nearby Forest of Mendip and King John's Royal Hunting Lodge in the village of Axbridge are further clues to the one-time importance of hunting in the area.

King's Wood is part of the Crook Peak to Shute Shelve Site of Special Scientific Interest (SSSI). It is rich in wildlife, with a varied and interesting ground flora that indicate continuous woodland cover over a long period of time.

The woods support a wide variety of birds such as great tits and blue tits, nuthatches, robin and songthrush, along with insects such as spiders, beetles and butterflies, mammals such as badgers and deer and a whole range of fungi, ferns, mosses and lichens which mostly favour the fairly damp conditions of woodlands.

Plants such as wood anemones, bluebells, wild garlic and dog's mercury are common, as are trees and shrubs such as small-leaved lime, oak, beech, field maple, ash, whitebeam, hazel and guelder rose.

Adrian Boots

The roe deer's comeback

Present in the UK since the last Ice Age, the elegant **roe deer** (*Capreolus capreolus*) was once considered the preserve of royalty, its meat a delicacy only to be served at the royal table. Excessive hunting and woodland clearance drove it close to extinction a couple of hundred years ago, but the growth of forestry and more enlightened attitudes to conservation have brought it back and there are now thought to be at least 500,000 roe in the UK.

Chris Newton

The roebuck is distinguished from the doe by its larger size and its dainty antlers, which give an indication of age – there are up to three tines (points) on each antler. The colour of both sexes changes very noticeably with the season, from a rich reddish-brown coat in the summer to a drab brownish-grey in winter. The rear view of a roe – the only one the careless walker is likely to get – reveals a striking creamy-white rump patch.

The roe can run like the wind and leap high fences to escape predators. It is not as defenceless as it looks – the little hooves have sharp points which can inflict serious injury if the animal is cornered.

Roe deer tend to spend the daylight hours in cover, emerging at dusk to feed in open spaces. They browse off tree shoots and agricultural crops, which can cause economic pressures.

Illustration: Neil Ross

A year in the life of a roe deer

SPRING
- The females give birth during May and June
- They normally have 1 or 2 young or 'kids', sometimes 3.

SUMMER
- The breeding season or 'rut' occurs between mid July and mid August
- Males become more aggressive and maintain exclusive territories around one or more does
- Fights between bucks can lead to serious injury or death
- The winning male takes over both the loser's territory and his does
- Does call to bucks using a high-pitched piping call – the bucks respond with a rasping noise
- Bucks chase does until the they are ready to mate. Usually they mate with several females.

AUTUMN AND WINTER
- Although mating occurs in August, the fertilised egg does not implant for four months. The eggs begins to develop in January and the foetus takes five months to develop. Delayed implantation is likely to be an evolutionary adaptation to avoid giving birth during winter – badgers also use it.

Flowers of the ancient woods

Wood Anemone

(Anemone nemorosa) Widespread and locally abundant in woodland, coppices and hedgerows across most of the UK, the delicate wood anemone is a characteristic indicator of ancient woodland. The white flowers are solitary, sometimes with a tinge of pink or purple beneath, measuring 2-4cm across with 5-7 petal-like sepals. The leaves each have 3 much-divided and toothed lobes. The whole plant is poisonous.

Dog's Mercury

(Mercurialis perennis) The dog's mercury is another plant which goes by several different country names – dog's flower, dog's medicine, snake's food and snake's meat are all on the list.

It is a widespread and generally common perennial of woodlands in the UK. The upright stems carry oval, toothed leaves. Erect clusters of very small male and female flowers are found on separate plants and appear from February to April.

Other things to look out for at or near King's Wood

- Saxon manorial boundary
- Crook Peak and Wavering Down
- King John's Royal Hunting Lodge and Museum at Axbridge
- Cheddar Valley railway Local Nature Reserve

King's Wood

Distance: 4km (2½ miles).

Time: About 1-1½ hours.

Starting points: King's Wood car park, OS Grid Ref ST 421 560.

Terrain: Uneven bridleways with some short steep slopes. Some walking on lanes but mainly a level and easy walk.

Route: Take the bridleway through King's Wood (1) and once clear of the trees (2), walk down the short steep slope to the road at Cross. Walk left along the lane past the New Inn at Cross (3). Take care when crossing A38. Continue along Cross Lane and after a few yards, you will find the footpath next to the field gate (4). Walk along the hedge in the field and over the stile, then cross the road and walk along the lane to find the entrance to Strawberry Line (5) for a level and easy return walk (6). Continue through the tunnel under the road (7), then turn left through gate (8) and follow the footpath up through the meadow to return to the car park.

Waymarking: Look for the special waymark plaques wherever there are stiles, gates or changes of direction.

O.S.Map: Explorer 141: Cheddar Gorge & Mendip Hills West.

Other Information: Pubs in Cross: New Inn and White Hart and further pubs in Axbridge: Oak House, Lamb Hotel and Crown Inn. Village post office and stores in Axbridge.

Adrian Boots

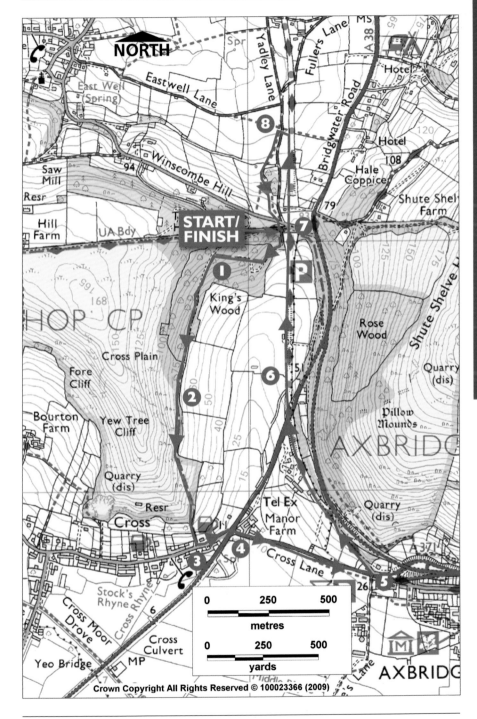

THREE PRIDDY DROVES:

Corridors for vulnerable wildlife

Hedges, ditches, fences, roadside verges or streams which connect two existing areas of habitat and enable species to move between them are known as wildlife corridors. These corridors are vital in allowing wildlife to enlarge existing ranges and colonise new areas.

In the Mendips, sheep and cattle droves often act as wildlife corridors. These droves were created to allow farmers to drive their animals from the fields to the local markets. They are like unsurfaced roadways through the landscape, wide enough for the animals to graze on passage and bordered by hedges or dry stone walls to stop them escaping.

These days farm animals travel by road, but the droves remain. Some have become public rights of way which allow better access to the countryside.

What does it take to make a wildlife corridor? Depending on the species, the key features will include shelter and protection from predators, a favourable microclimate, the presence of hibernation or overwintering sites, even breeding territory. Ideally it should be continuous.

While the droves around Priddy, such as Pelting, Dursdon & East Water Drove, are typically marked by dry stone walls, many are also bordered by shrubs such as hawthorn, blackthorn and elder. They provide a valuable habitat for plants, animals and insects. The top of the Mendip Plateau is quite exposed to the elements, and many species of flowering plants, ferns, lichens and mosses find refuge on the leeward side of the walls. Insects, reptiles and small mammals benefit from the sun traps created on the sunny sides.

Many vulnerable creatures such as small mammals, birds and lizards will keep to the shelter of the droves rather than crossing open fields where they risk predation. However, their enemies have had plenty of time to work this out – and some of them hunt around the droves, knowing their prey is more likely to be found there.

Mendip Hills AONB Service

Illustration: Neil Ross

Death on silent wings

One example is the **barn owl** *(Tyto alba)*, that beautiful, silent predator of unimproved meadows and farmland with plenty of cover. The owl, often known in the past as the white owl, is much paler than the other British species. It is most often spotted from a car, flying at low level beside a country lane in the late dusk as it hunts for small mammals.

There's no mistaking the barn owl's buff upper surfaces, flecked with pepper-and-salt markings, its white underparts and distinctive white heart-shaped face.

It hunts in open country, often along linear habitats such as field and woodland edges, riverbanks, roadside verges and of course, droves. It prefers traditional nesting sites such as holes in trees, old barns and outbuildings but may also adopt carefully-sited nestboxes.

Barn owls need rough grassland with good populations of rodents, especially mice, voles and shrews. The prey is normally swallowed whole. The fur, bones, teeth and feathers are then regurgitated in the form of large, black pellets. The barn owl is protected under the Wildlife and Countryside Act, 1981.

Mendip Hills AONB Service

Barn owl facts

- The hearing of a barn owl is so acute that it can find its tiny prey by sound alone, even on the darkest night
- One ear is positioned higher than the other, to increase sound reception – the left ear captures sounds from below, while the right looks after those from above
- The feathers around the owl's dished face are shaped to focus sound to its ears
- Barn Owls have very long legs and long toes and talons, to help them catch prey through long grass
- On average a wild barn owl eats around 4 small mammals per night – over 1400 a year
- Barn Owls screech, rather than hoot (only the male tawny owl hoots)
- They lay four to seven white eggs over two to three days. Incubation lasts 30-31 days and the young hatch at 2-3 day intervals
- The young birds fly at 50 to 55 days
- In a good year, two broods may be reared
- In the wild, Barn Owls rarely live longer than 3 years – in captivity, however, they have been known to make it to 20.

Plants to look out for

Lichens and mosses

Study the limestone rocks and walls of the Mendips and one of the first things you'll notice is how many of the plants are not actually rooted in the ground.

We can thank the lichens and mosses for this – the lichens are the first to colonise bare rock, followed by a succession of species of moss. These more primitive plants pave the way for vascular plants such as grasses and flowers by breaking down the surface. This creates a substrate which can sustain flowers such as biting stonecrop *(Sedum acre)*, wall pennywort *(Umbilicus rupestris)* and red valerian *(Centranthus ruber)*.

The common lizard

Only two species of legged lizard are native to Britain and only one, the so-called **common lizard** *(Lacerta vivipara)*, is widespread – the much more localised sand lizard is restricted to a few carefully-managed areas of dry heathland. The common lizard is also known as the

viviparous lizard, because it gives birth to live young – most reptiles produce eggs. As befits a British lizard, this species is more tolerant of cold and damp than most of its relatives, and can be found (if you look hard enough) in almost any kind of well-established rough terrain such as unmanaged grassland, heathland and on acid bogs, where it hunts its invertebrate prey among the ground vegetation. It is small – rarely more than about 14cm in length – and its cryptic striped and speckled fawnish or greenish colouring makes it hard to spot.

What to look out for near Pelting, Dursdon & East Water Droves

• Sheep Hurdles on Priddy Green
• Ebbor Gorge National Nature Reserve
• Milton Lodge gardens
• Priddy Nine Barrows – Bronze Age round barrows.

Priddy Droves

Distance: 8km (4.5 miles).

Time: About 2-2½ hours.

Starting point: Priddy village green, OS Grid Ref ST 526 509.

Terrain: A mixture of uneven droves, tracks, footpaths and roads, but overall fairly level with only gentle slopes.

Route: From the village green **(1)**, head south along Pelting Drove **(2)** for just over 1km until you find the entrance to Dursdon Drove on your left **(3)**. Follow the Drove for 2km, until it is bisected by the Monarch's Way **(4)**. Turn left and follow the Monarch's Way north (please be aware of grazing animals) until you meet the Wells Road **(5)**. Turn left, leaving the Monarch's Way and walk for 200m and then turn right along East Water Lane Drove **(6)**. At the end of the lane, turn left onto Nine Barrows Lane **(7)** and walk to the crossroads. Turn left on to the lane leading back to Priddy. The route can be extended to include the rest of Dursdon Drove, Ebbor Gorge and or the Priddy Mineries.

Waymarking: Look for the special waymark plaques wherever there are stiles, gates or changes of direction. This route follows part of the West Mendip Way and the Monarch's Way.

O.S.Map: Explorer 141: Cheddar Gorge & Mendip Hills West.

Other Information:
Parking in Priddy. Parking at Ebbor Wood and Pelting Drove.
Three pubs in/near Priddy:
Queen Victoria, New Inn and Hunters Lodge Inn.
Annual events in Priddy:
Sheep Fair and Folk Festival.

Mendip Hills AONB Service

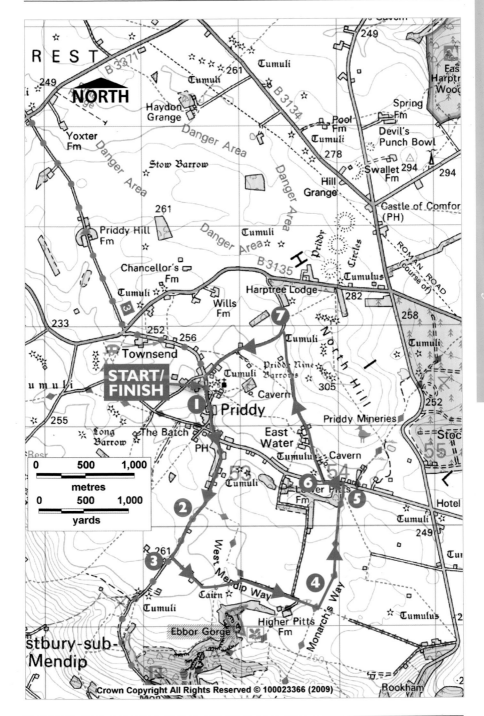

Acknowledgements

Author:	Adrian Boots
Additional material:	Chris Newton *(pp37-38 Lichens & Mosses, Common Lizard)*
	Neil Ross *(p3 Walking in Safety)*
Editor:	Chris Newton
Photography:	Steve Bond
	Adrian Boots
	Paul Glendell/Natural England
	Jim Hallet/Countryside Agency
	Richard Law
	Mendip Hills AONB Service
	Chris Newton
	Peter Roworth/Natural England
	Peter Wakely/Natural England
Designer:	Neil Ross/Four Square Design (01275 371913)
Illustrations:	Neil Ross
Published by:	Mendip Hills AONB Service

© Mendip Hills AONB Service 2009

Mendip Hills AONB Service   **ISBN - Wild Walks 978-0-9559110-1-9**

While every care has been taken to ensure the accuracy of the route directions, we cannot accept responsibility for errors or omissions, or for changes in the details given. The countryside is not static and is subject to changes to field boundaries, footpath routes and property ownership resulting in the closure or diversion of concessionary paths. We have taken all reasonable steps to ensure these walks are safe and achievable by walkers with a reasonable level of fitness. However, all outdoor activities involve a degree of risk and the publishers accept no responsibility for any injuries sustained to readers whilst following these walks.

Area of Outstanding
Natural Beauty

Mendip Hills AONB Service
Charterhouse Centre
nr Blagdon
Bristol BS40 7XR

www.mendiphillsaonb.org.uk
E-mail: mendiphills@somerset.gov.uk
Telephone: 01761 462338

Working together for equalities
This document is also available in Braille, large print, on tape or on disc and we can translate it into different languages. We can provide a member of staff to discuss the details.

RNID typetalk

This book is printed on Howard Smith Greencoat Velvet paper containing 80% recycled fibre. The remaining 20% virgin pulp is TCF (Totally Chlorine Free).